# NEW WEIGHT WATCHERS FREESTYLE COOKBOOK

## BY EVA DAVIS

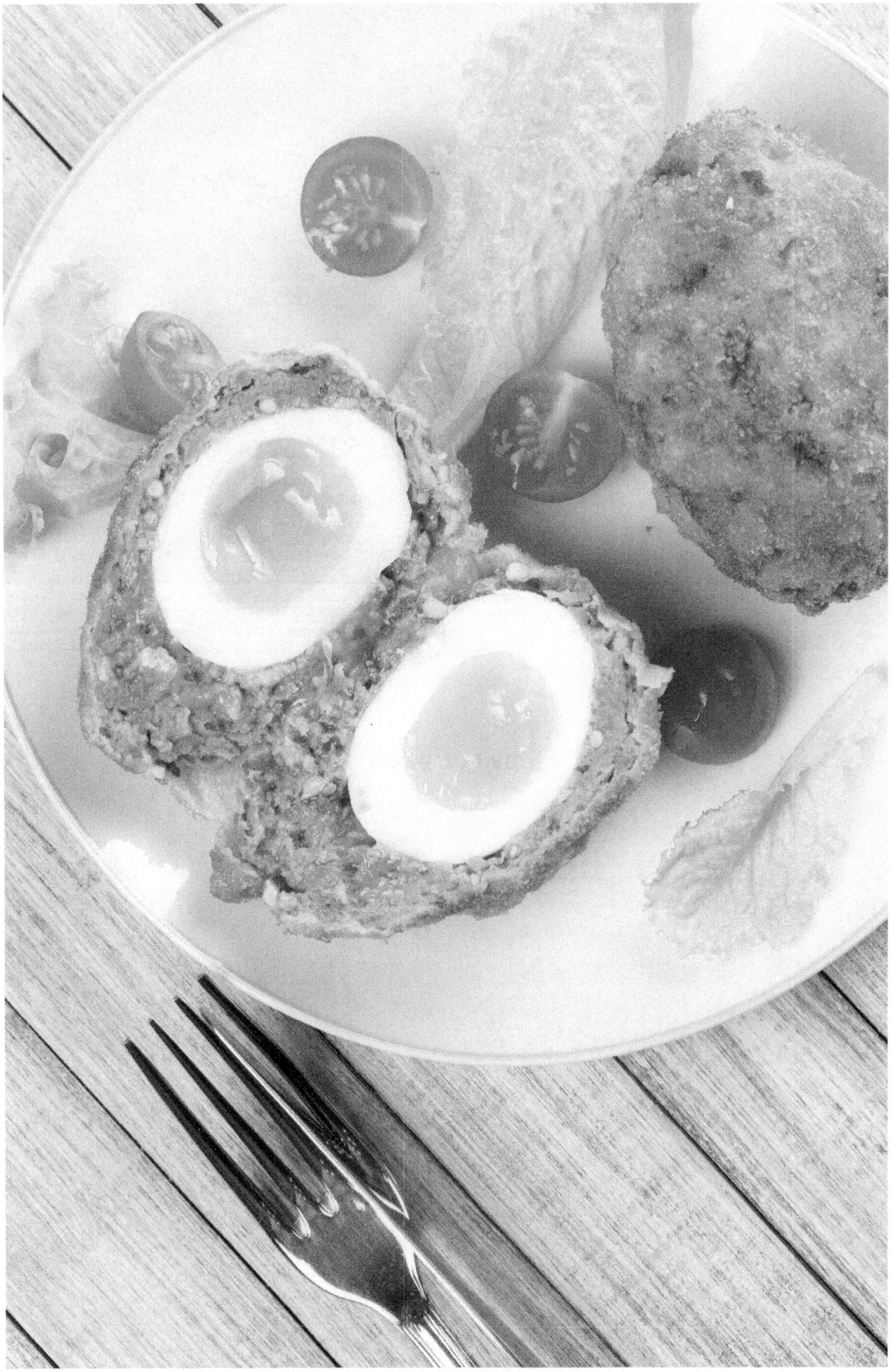

© **Copyright 2020 by Eva Davis - All rights reserved.**

Disclaimer Notice:

Please note the information contained within this document is for educational and entertainment purposes only. Every attempt has been made to provide accurate, up to date and reliable, complete information. No warranties of any kind are expressed or implied. Readers acknowledge that the author is not engaging in the rendering of legal, financial, medical or professional advice. By reading this document, the reader agrees that under no circumstances are we responsible for any losses, direct or indirect, which are incurred as a result of the use of information contained within this document, including, but not limited to, errors, omissions, or inaccuracies.

Legal Notice:

This book is copyright protected. This is only for personal use. You cannot amend, distribute, sell, use, quote or paraphrase any part or the content within this book without the consent of the author or copyright owner. Legal action will be pursued if this is breached.

## TABLE OF CONTENTS

**CHAPTER 1: WEIGHT WATCHERS FREESTYLE PROGRAM** .................................. 8
    THE FREESTYLE PROGRAM AND SMARTPOINTS .................................. 8
    RESTRICTED FOODS .................................. 8
    FOODS WITH ZERO SMARTPOINTS .................................. 9

**CHAPTER 2: BREAKFAST RECIPES** .................................. 13
    BACON EGG MUFFINS .................................. 13
    BROCCOLI EGG MUFFINS .................................. 15
    PEANUT BUTTER OATS .................................. 17
    APPLE HONEY OATS .................................. 18
    CHEESE EGG BREAKFAST .................................. 20
    CLASSIC CRANBERRY OATMEAL .................................. 22

**CHAPTER 3: FREESTYLE SOUPS & STEWS** .................................. 23
    STEAK BEAN SOUP .................................. 23
    CHICKEN CORN SPINACH SOUP .................................. 25
    TOMATO HERB SOUP .................................. 27
    HEALTHY CAULIFLOWER SOUP .................................. 29
    SHRIMP RICE PORRIDGE .................................. 31
    CHICKEN MUSHROOM STEW .................................. 33

**CHAPTER 4: CHICKEN & POULTRY** .................................. 35
    SOY HONEY CHICKEN .................................. 35
    CLASSIC BROCCOLI CHICKEN .................................. 37
    CHICKEN EGG LUNCHBOX .................................. 39
    TURKEY TOMATINO .................................. 40
    HONEYED CHICKEN CRISP .................................. 42
    VEGETABLE CHICKEN WITH BROWN RICE .................................. 44
    POTATO CHICKEN ROAST .................................. 46
    COCONUT CURRY CHICKEN .................................. 48
    GARLIC SALSA CHICKEN .................................. 50
    MEXICAN BEAN CHICKEN .................................. 51

**CHAPTER 5: PORK, BEEF & LAMB** .................................. 53
    CLASSIC ROSEMARY ROAST .................................. 53

Honeyed Beef Tenderloin.................................................................54
Asian Style Pork Veggies..................................................................56
Beef Stuffed Zucchini .......................................................................58
Beef Burger Patties ..........................................................................60
Zucchini Chili Beef ...........................................................................62
Beef Burger Patties ..........................................................................64
Beef Parmesan Noodles ..................................................................66
Slow Baked Beef Vegetables ...........................................................68
Baked Mustard Pork Chops .............................................................69
Beef Lettuce Burgers .......................................................................70
Creamy Pork Chops .........................................................................72
Beef Broccoli Dinner ........................................................................74
Roast Taco Wraps ...........................................................................76
Grilled Spiced Chops .......................................................................77

**CHAPTER 6: FISH & SEAFOOD** ......................................................79
Baked Herbed Salmon .....................................................................79
Creamed Halibut ..............................................................................81
Classic Crab Cakes .........................................................................83
Classic Ginger Garlic Fish ................................................................85
Tuna Mayonnaise Sandwich .............................................................87
Saucy Carrot Shrimp ........................................................................88
Wholesome Salmon Vegetables ......................................................90
Avocado Tuna Salad ........................................................................92
Herbed Seafood Meal ......................................................................93
Avocado Crab Salad ........................................................................95
Potato Mayo Fish..............................................................................97
Tuna Cranberry Salad ......................................................................99
Salmon Asparagus Treat ................................................................101

**CHAPTER 7: MEATLESS** ...............................................................103
Kale Quinoa Salad .........................................................................103
Egg Cheese Sandwich ...................................................................105
Squash Cheese Risotto .................................................................107
Broccoli Cauliflower Curry ..............................................................109
Bean Red Onion Salad ..................................................................111
Zucchini Cheese Noodles ..............................................................113

Potato Buttermilk Appetizer .......................................................... 114
Orange Glazed Potatoes .............................................................. 116
Broccoli Spinach Greens ............................................................. 118
Mango Arugula Salad ................................................................... 119
Cream Mayo Corn ........................................................................ 120

**CHAPTER 8: DESSERTS** ............................................................. 121
Apple Yogurt Parfait ...................................................................... 121
Cheesy Cracker Cups .................................................................. 123
Cream Mango Chill ....................................................................... 124
Blueberry Lemon Muffins ............................................................. 125
Applesauce Bean Brownies ......................................................... 127
Pumpkin Cake Muffins .................................................................. 129

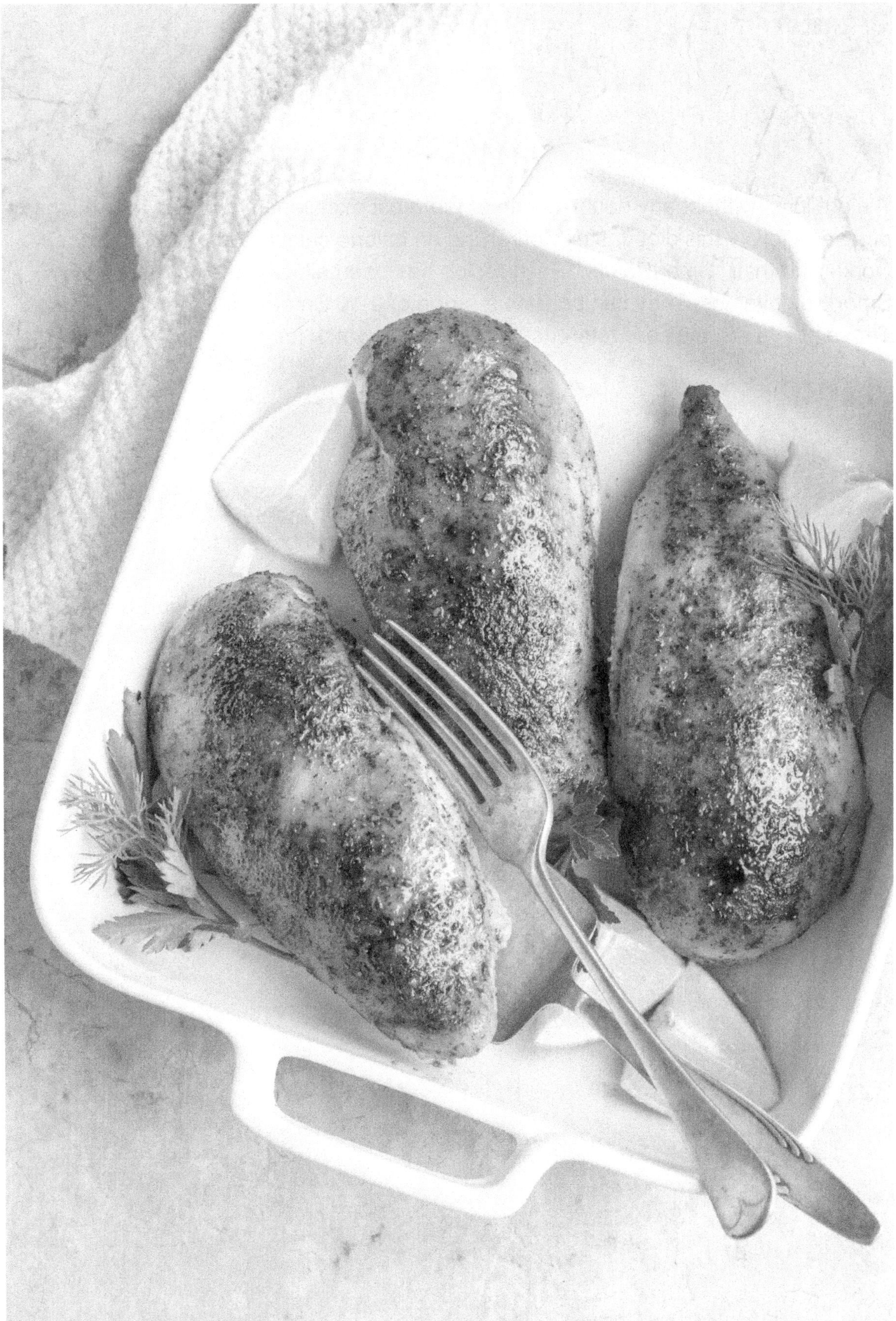

## Chapter 1: Weight Watchers Freestyle Program

**The Freestyle Program and SmartPoints**

Weight loss, without any doubt, is one of the most excellent motivators for millions of people to follow this diet. Instead of relying on calorie calculations, this program works with their "SmartPoints." Each recipe has been allocated to its respective SmartPoint values. They can be from a range of 0-10 SmartPoints per serving. Those points are the core reference for dieters to watch for.

**Restricted Foods**

- Commercially fried foods, packaged snacks, and commercial bakery items
- All sweetened commercial drinks, fruit juices, and beverages
- All types of processed meats
- All other types of sweetened products such as sweetened Yogurts, sweetened canned products, etc.

# Foods with Zero SmartPoints

- Arrowroot
- Apricots
- Asparagus
- Arugula
- Artichokes
- Artichoke hearts
- Applesauce, unsweetened
- Apples
- Banana
- Bamboo shoots
- Beans, canned
- Beets
- Broccoli slaw
- Broccoli
- Beans (all varieties)
- Berries (all varieties)
- Brussels sprouts
- Calamari
- Cabbage (all varieties)
- Caviar
- Cauliflower
- Chard (all varieties)
- Cherries
- Chicken breast or tenderloin (with bone or boneless)
- Celery
- Carrots
- Cantaloupe
- Chicken breast, fat-free and ground
- Cucumber
- Cranberries
- Coleslaw mix
- Collards
- Corn (yellow, kernels, baby ears, white, on the cob)
- Dates, fresh
- Daikon
- Dragon fruit
- Egg substitutes
- Edamame (pods or shelled)
- Eggs, whole

- Egg whites
- Endive
- Eggplant
- Fennel
- Escarole
- Figs, fresh
- Fish (smoked and all other varieties)
- Fruit, unsweetened
- Fruit salad
- Ginger root
- Garlic
- Grapes
- Grapefruit
- Guavas
- Greens (all varieties)
- Strawberries
- Honeydew melon
- Hearts of palm
- Jerk chicken breast
- Jackfruit
- Jicama
- Kumquats
- Kohlrabi
- Kiwifruit
- Lemon zest
- Lemon
- Leeks
- Lime zest
- Lentils
- Lime
- Lettuce (all varieties)
- Melon balls
- Mangoes
- Lychees
- Mung dal
- Mung bean sprouts
- Mushrooms (all varieties)
- Mushroom caps
- Nori seaweed
- Nectarines
- Oranges (all varieties)

- Onions
- Okra
- Pea shoots
- Passion fruit
- Parsley
- Papayas
- Pears
- Peaches
- Peas (all varieties)
- Peas & carrots
- Pickles, unsweetened
- Pomegranate seeds
- Persimmons
- Peas & carrots
- Pineapples
- Pumpkin puree, unsweetened
- Pomelo
- Plums
- Pomegranates
- Pumpkin
- Radishes
- Radicchio
- Rutabagas
- Raspberries
- Salad, side without dressing
- Sashimi (all varieties)
- Salsa, fat-free (all varieties)
- Scallions
- Salad, mixed greens
- Salad, tossed without dressing
- Shallots
- Squash (all varieties)
- Sauerkraut
- Seaweed
- Shellfish (all varieties)
- Succotash
- Strawberries
- Sprouts (all varieties)
- Spinach
- Tangerines
- Turkey breast, fat-free and ground

- Turkey breast or tenderloin (with bone or skinless, boneless)
- Turnips
- Tangelo
- Tomatillos
- Tofu (all varieties)
- Tomato sauce
- Tomato puree
- Tomatoes (all varieties)
- Watercress
- Yogurt, plain, fat-free, unsweetened, including Greek Yogurt
- Vegetables, stir fry
- Vegetables, mixed
- Watermelon

# Chapter 2: Breakfast Recipes

## Bacon Egg Muffins

**Prep Time:** 8-10 min.

**Cooking Time:** 25-30 min.

**Number of Servings:** 3

**SMARTPOINTS PER SERVING: 4**

**Ingredients**:

- ¼ cup skim milk
- 6 egg whites
- 6 eggs
- ½ cup shredded part-skim mozzarella
- Pepper and salt as per taste
- 1 zucchini, cut to dice
- 6 pieces turkey bacon, chop into small pieces

**Directions**:

1. Preheat an oven to 375°F.
2. Spray 6 muffins with cooking spray.
3. Take a skillet or saucepan (medium size preferable); heat it over a medium cooking flame.
4. Add some cooking spray and heat it.
5. Add the bacon and cook until crisp for 5-6 minutes. Add the bacon to a plate and discard bacon fat.
6. Add the zucchini to the saucepan and sauté until tender for 4-5 minutes. Add with the bacon.
7. Take a mixing bowl (either medium or large size), crack and whisk the eggs. Season as needed.
8. Mix in the milk, cheese, zucchini, and bacon.
9. Add muffin tins; bake for 20 minutes. Serve warm.

**Nutritional Values (Per Serving):**

**Calories – 246**

**Fat – 14g**

**Saturated Fats – 6g**

**Trans Fats - 0g**

**Carbohydrates – 6g**

**Fiber – 1g**

**Sodium – 754mg**

**Protein – 27g**

# Broccoli Egg Muffins

**Prep Time: 8-10 min.**

**Cooking Time: 13-15 min.**

**Number of Servings: 6**

**SMARTPOINTS PER SERVING: 4**

**Ingredients:**

- 2 cups broccoli, steamed and chopped into small pieces
- Pepper and salt as per taste
- ½ tablespoon Dijon mustard
- 2 green onions, chop into small pieces
- ¾ cup shredded cheddar cheese, reduced fat
- 4 egg whites
- 8 eggs

**Directions:**

1. Preheat an oven to 350°F.
2. Spray 12 muffins with cooking spray.
3. Take a mixing bowl (either medium or large size), crack and whisk the eggs. Mix in the pepper, salt, mustard, and egg whites.
4. Mix in the cheese, green onions, and broccoli.
5. Add the mix into muffin tins. Bake for 12 minutes or until puffs up.
6. Serve warm.

**Nutritional Values (Per Serving):**

**Calories – 184**

**Fat – 9g**

**Saturated Fats – 4g**

**Trans Fats - 0g**

**Carbohydrates – 4g**

**Fiber – 1g**

**Sodium – 312mg**

**Protein – 16g**

# Peanut Butter Oats

**Prep Time:** 8-10 min.

**Cooking Time:** 0 min.

**Number of Servings:** 1

**SMARTPOINTS PER SERVING:** 7

**Ingredients:**

- ¾ cup almond milk
- 1 tablespoon jam, sugar-free
- 1 tablespoon peanut butter
- ½ cup old-fashioned oats

**Directions:**

1. Take a mixing bowl (either medium or large size), add and mix in the ingredients except the jam in the bowl to mix well with each other.
2. Cover the bowl and set in the fridge overnight.
3. Take out in the morning and add a jam on top. Serve.

**Nutritional Values (Per Serving):**

**Calories** – 226

**Fat** – 8g

**Saturated Fats** – 1g

**Trans Fats** - 0g

**Carbohydrates** – 32g

**Fiber** – 7g

**Sodium** – 97mg

**Protein** – 9g

**Apple Honey Oats**

**Prep Time:** 8-10 min.

**Cooking Time:** 10-15 min.

**Number of Servings:** 4

**SMARTPOINTS PER SERVING: 4**

**Ingredients:**

- 1 teaspoon vanilla extract
- 1 gala apple, peeled and cut to dice
- 2 tablespoons honey
- 1 cup milk
- 1/8 tsp salt
- 1 teaspoon cinnamon
- 2 cups water
- ½ cup steel cut oats

**Directions:**

1. Take a skillet or saucepan (medium size preferable); heat it over a medium cooking flame.
2. Add the vanilla, honey, milk, and water and boil the mix.
3. Add the oatmeal and apples and mix well.
4. Turn down the cooking flame to low setting; cover the saucepan or skillet and let the mix simmer for about 8-10 minutes (stir in between).
5. Stir in the salt and cinnamon; cook for 1-2 minutes. Serve warm.

**Nutritional Values (Per Serving):**

**Calories - 161**

**Fat – 2g**

**Saturated Fats – 1g**

**Trans Fats - 0g**

**Carbohydrates – 26g**

**Fiber – 7g**

**Sodium – 43mg**

**Protein – 5g**

## Cheese Egg Breakfast

**Prep Time:** 10 min.

**Cooking Time:** 10 min.

**Number of Servings:** 4

**SMARTPOINTS PER SERVING: 5**

**Ingredients**:

2 tablespoons green onion, chopped

2 whole large egg

4 large egg white

1/8 teaspoon hot pepper sauce, or to taste

½ cup cooked lean ham, diced

1/8 teaspoon black pepper

¼ teaspoon salt

¼ cup parmesan cheese

**Directions**:

1. In a mixing bowl, beat the egg whites.
2. In another bowl, beat the whole eggs. Add the egg white and stir.
3. Add the green onion, salt, pepper, and hot sauce; combine well.
4. In a saucepan or skillet, heat some vegetable oil over medium heat setting.
5. Add the mixture and stir-cook for 1-2 minutes.
6. Add the ham and cheese; stir-cook until the cheese melts.
7. Serve warm.

**Nutritional Values (Per Serving):**

Calories: 118
Fat: 4.5g
Saturated Fat: 2g
Trans Fat: 0g
Carbohydrates: 6g
Fiber: 1g
Sodium: 467mg
Protein: 10g

# Classic Cranberry Oatmeal

**Prep Time:** 5 min.

**Cooking Time:** 5 min.

**Number of Servings:** 1

**SMARTPOINTS PER SERVING: 3**

**Ingredients:**

½ cup unsweetened applesauce

3 tablespoons uncooked oatmeal

1 tablespoon dried cranberry

½ cup water

1/8 teaspoon ground cinnamon

**Directions:**

1. Take a saucepan, add the water, applesauce, and cranberries. Stir the mixture.
2. Heat over the medium cooking flame until the berries are softened for 3-4 minutes.
3. Add the oatmeal and stir-cook for 2-3 minutes until the oatmeal thickens.
4. Serve topped with cinnamon.

**Nutritional Values (Per Serving):**

Calories: 95
Fat: 0.5g
Saturated Fat: 0g
Trans Fat: 0g
Carbohydrates: 18g
Fiber: 4g
Sodium: 21mg
Protein: 1g

# Chapter 3: Freestyle Soups & Stews

## Steak Bean Soup

**Prep Time:** 8-10 min.

**Cooking Time:** 25-30 min.

**Number of Servings:** 8

**SMARTPOINTS PER SERVING: 1**

**Ingredients:**

- ½ cup chop into small pieces, onions
- 1 teaspoon Italian seasoning mix
- ½ teaspoon olive oil
- ½ pound lean round steak, sliced
- ¼ teaspoon garlic salt
- ¼ teaspoon pepper
- 1 can tomatoes, diced
- ½ cup chop into small pieces, carrots
- 2 ½ cups shredded cabbage
- ¼ cup snipped parsley
- 1 can white kidney beans, rinsed and drained
- 2 cans beef broth, fat-free and low-sodium

**Directions:**

1. Take a skillet or saucepan (medium size preferable); heat it over a medium cooking flame.
2. Add the oil and heat it.
3. Stir in the meat and onions. Stir-cook for 3 minutes.
4. Mix in the seasoning mix, garlic, salt, and pepper; cook for 2 minutes.
5. Mix and stir the tomatoes, carrots, kidney beans and broth.
6. Boil and allow to simmer for 20 minutes.
7. Add the cabbages and parsley; simmer for 5 more minutes.
8. Serve warm.

**Nutritional Values (Per Serving):**

**Calories – 137**

**Fat – 2g**

**Saturated Fats – 1g**

**Trans Fats - 0g**

**Carbohydrates – 15g**

**Fiber – 4g**

**Sodium – 654mg**

**Protein – 12g**

# Chicken Corn Spinach Soup

**Prep Time:** 8-10 min.

**Cooking Time:** 70-80 min.

**Number of Servings:** 8

**SMARTPOINTS PER SERVING: 3**

**Ingredients:**

- 4 cups baby spinach
- 1 white onion, cut to dice
- 3 cloves minced roasted garlic
- 1 pound boneless skinless chicken breasts, roasted and shredded
- 2 cups frozen corn, thawed
- 1 yellow bell pepper, cut to dice
- 3 cups chicken broth, low-sodium
- 1 tablespoon cumin
- 1 tablespoon salt
- 3 poblano peppers, roasted and cut to dice
- 5 cups water
- 1 teaspoon black pepper
- 1 cup fat-free sour cream

**Directions:**

1. Take a cooking pot or deep saucepan (medium size preferable); heat it over a medium cooking flame.
2. Combine all Ingredients, except for the sour cream in the pot. Mix until well-combined.
3. Boil the mix; let the mix simmer for about 60 minutes (stir in between).
4. Mix in the cream and continue cooking for 10 minutes.
5. Serve warm.

**Nutritional Values (Per Serving):**

**Calories - 141**

**Fat – 3g**

**Saturated Fats – 0g**

**Trans Fats - 0g**

**Carbohydrates – 14g**

**Fiber – 2g**

**Sodium – 194mg**

**Protein – 15g**

# Tomato Herb Soup

**Prep Time:** 8-10 min.

**Cooking Time:** 15 min.

**Number of Servings:** 4

**SMARTPOINTS PER SERVING: 5**

**Ingredients:**

- ½ cup chop into small pieces, onions
- 1 stalk celery, chop into small pieces
- 3 tablespoons olive oil
- 2 cloves of garlic, minced
- 1 cup chicken broth, fat-free and low-sodium
- 1 cup skim milk
- 5 fresh basil leaves
- 1 14-ounce can tomato puree
- Pepper and salt as per taste
- 1 tablespoon cornstarch + 2 tablespoons water

**Directions:**

1. Mix the cornstarch with water in a bowl.
2. Add the onions and celery in a food processor and pulse until smooth.
3. Take a skillet or saucepan (medium size preferable); heat it over a medium cooking flame.
4. Add the oil and heat it.
5. Add the onion puree. Stir-cook for 3 minutes until translucent.
6. Add the garlic, broth, and tomato puree.
7. Season as per taste. Boil and simmer for 5 minutes.
8. Whisk in the milk, basil leaves, and cornstarch slurry; simmer for another 5 minutes.
9. Serve warm.

**Nutritional Values (Per Serving):**

**Calories – 164**

**Fat – 10g**

**Saturated Fats – 1g**

**Trans Fats - 0g**

**Carbohydrates – 13g**

**Fiber – 2g**

**Sodium – 62mg**

**Protein – 5g**

# Healthy Cauliflower Soup

**Prep Time:** 10-15 min.

**Cooking Time:** 2 min.

**Number of Servings:** 2

**SMARTPOINTS PER SERVING: 1**

**Ingredients:**

1 large head cauliflower, cut into florets

1 tablespoon butter

3 tablespoons flour

½ teaspoon dried basil

1 teaspoon parsley

2 tablespoons olive oil

1 small white onion, sliced

6 cups chicken or vegetable stock

1 bay leaf

1 tablespoon fish sauce

Ground black pepper and salt to taste

**Directions:**

1. In a cooking pot or deep saucepan, heat the butter over medium heat setting.
2. Add the flour and stir well. Add the olive oil, onion, and cauliflower; stir-cook for about 4-5 minutes.
3. Add the chicken stock. Bring to a boil.
4. Add the bay leaf. Partially cover and allow to simmer for about 25 minutes over the low stove flame.
5. Blend the mixture in a blender and add back to the pot. Mix in the fish sauce. Season to taste with salt and ground black pepper.
6. Serve warm.

**Nutritional Values (Per Serving):**

Calories: 274
Fat: 18g
Saturated Fat: 5.5g
Trans Fat: 0g
Carbohydrates: 22g
Fiber: 7g
Sodium: 857mg
Protein: 19g

# Shrimp Rice Porridge

**Prep Time: 10-15 min.**

**Cooking Time: 7 min.**

**Number of Servings: 4**

**SMARTPOINTS PER SERVING: 3**

**Ingredients**:

1 cup tomatoes, chopped

3 cups chicken stock

¼ cup shrimp, deboned and chopped

1 cup white rice

2 cups okra, cut into small pieces

1 teaspoon dried basil

½ teaspoon dried thyme

1 teaspoon fish sauce

1 tablespoon butter

1 clove garlic

1 large onion, diced

**Directions**:

1. In a cooking pot or deep saucepan, heat ½ tablespoon butter over medium heat setting.
2. Sauté the garlic until it becomes softened.
3. Add the shrimp and cook for 2-3 minutes. Set aside the mixture.
4. Add the remaining butter. Sauté the onions until it becomes softened and translucent.
5. Add the tomatoes and stir-cook for about 3-4 minutes.
6. Add the rice and stir-cook for 2 minutes. Add the chicken stock. Cook until the rice is cooked well.
7. Mix in the shrimp mixture and okra; stir-cook for about 2-3 minutes.
8. Season with the herbs, fish sauce, salt, and black pepper. Serve warm.

**Nutritional Values (Per Serving):**

Calories: 235
Fat: 4g
Saturated Fat: 2g
Trans Fat: 0g
Carbohydrates: 23g
Fiber: 3.5g
Sodium: 528mg
Protein: 6g

# Chicken Mushroom Stew

**Prep Time: 10 min.**

**Cooking Time: 10-15 min.**

**Number of Servings: 4**

**SMARTPOINTS PER SERVING: 4**

**Ingredients**:

2 tablespoons flour

1 tablespoon butter

2 cups chicken stock

3 cups leftover roasted chicken fillets, cubed

1 (12-14 ounce) can button mushroom

3 tablespoons soy sauce

1 teaspoon brown sugar, optional

**Directions**:

1. In a mixing bowl (medium-large size), add soy sauce, brown sugar, and chicken stock. Combine well.
2. In a cooking pot or deep saucepan, heat the butter over medium heat setting.
3. Add the flour and stir to combine. Add the chicken stock mixture.
4. Slowly boil the mixture; cover and allow to simmer until the mixture thickens over the low stove flame.
5. Add the mushroom and chicken. Season to taste with salt and ground black pepper.
6. Stir-cook for about 2 minutes. Serve warm.

**Nutritional Values (Per Serving):**

Calories: 143
Fat: 6.5g
Saturated Fat: 3g
Trans Fat: 0g
Carbohydrates: 11.5g
Fiber: 1g
Sodium: 563mg
Protein: 11.5g

# CHAPTER 4: CHICKEN & POULTRY

## Soy Honey Chicken

**Prep Time:** 15 min.

**Cooking Time:** 20 min.

**Number of Servings:** 4

**SMARTPOINTS PER SERVING: 6**

**Ingredients**:

4 (6-7 ounce) chicken breast fillet, pounded

1 cup white onions, diced

1 ½ tablespoon tomato ketchup

½ tablespoon soy sauce

¼ cup tamari or fish sauce

Juice of ½ orange

1 thumb size ginger, peeled and grated

2 cloves garlic, minced

1 tablespoon brown sugar

2 tablespoon honey

1 tablespoon cornstarch mixed with ½ tablespoon water

Ground black pepper and salt to taste

1 teaspoon sesame oil

1 tablespoon olive oil

1 tablespoon sesame seeds

**Directions**:

1. Season the chicken with ground black pepper and salt to taste. Set aside for 5-10 minutes.

2. In a cooking pot or deep saucepan, heat the oil over medium heat setting.
3. Stir-cook chicken until evenly brown for 2-3 minutes per side.
4. Take a greased baking dish and place the chicken in it.
5. In the pan, sauté the onions until translucent. Add the garlic and cook for 1 minute.
6. Add remaining ingredients except for the cornstarch slurry. Season with ground black pepper and salt to taste.
7. Boil the mixture and add the cornstarch slurry and stir until the sauce thickens. Take it off heat. Pour the mixture over the chicken.
8. Preheat an oven to 350°F. Bake for 15 minutes.
9. Add the sesame oil on top and sprinkle with toasted sesame seeds. Serve with cabbages.

**Nutritional Values (Per Serving):**

Calories: 362
Fat: 13g
Saturated Fat: 1.5g
Trans Fat: 0g
Carbohydrates: 25g
Fiber: 3.5g
Sodium: 563mg
Protein: 42.5g

# Classic Broccoli Chicken

**Prep Time: 10-15 min.**

**Cooking Time: 15 min.**

**Number of Servings: 4 (1 cup per serving)**

**SMARTPOINTS PER SERVING: 3**

**Ingredients**:

12 ounce uncooked boneless skinless chicken breasts, thinly sliced

2 teaspoons olive oil

2 tablespoons all-purpose flour

½ teaspoon table salt

¼ teaspoon black pepper

1 ½ cup chicken broth, fat-free reduced sodium

2 teaspoons lemon zest

2 tablespoons fresh parsley, chopped

2 teaspoons minced garlic

2 ½ cups uncooked broccoli florets

1 tablespoon fresh lemon juice

**Directions**:

1. In a mixing bowl (medium-large size), add the 1 1/2 tablespoons flour, 1/4 teaspoon black pepper, and salt. Combine well.
2. Add the chicken and coat well.
3. In a saucepan or skillet, heat the oil over medium heat setting.
4. Add the chicken and stir-cook for 2-3 minutes on each side to evenly brown. Set aside.
5. Add 1 cup broth and garlic; boil the mixture with high heat. Add the broccoli and cook for 1 minutes.
6. Combine remaining broth, 1/4 teaspoon salt, and 1/2 tablespoons flour in another bowl. Add the mixture in the pan and simmer the mixture until the broccoli turns tender and sauce thickens.
7. Add the zest and chicken; combine well. Mix in the lemon juice.

8. Serve warm with the parsley on top.

**Nutritional Values (Per Serving):**

Calories: 193
Fat: 8.5g
Saturated Fat: 1g
Trans Fat: 0g
Carbohydrates: 11g
Fiber: 3g
Sodium: 358mg
Protein: 26g

## Chicken Egg Lunchbox

**Prep Time:** 10-15 min.

**Cooking Time:** 0 min.

**Number of Servings:** 4

**SMARTPOINTS PER SERVING: 0**

**Ingredients:**

4 cups cooked chicken, shredded

4 hardboiled eggs

2 sliced apples

2 cups grapes

1 cup sliced cucumbers

1 cup diced peppers

Salt and black pepper to taste

Chopped parsley to taste

Yogurt dip to serve (optional)

**Directions:**

1. In a lunchbox, combine all the ingredients and season with salt and pepper.
2. Add chopped parsley on top and serve with the yogurt dip.

**Nutritional Values (Per Serving):**

Calories: 272
Fat: 14.5g
Saturated Fat: 4g
Trans Fat: 0g
Carbohydrates: 31g
Fiber: 3g
Sodium: 184mg
Protein: 42g

## Turkey Tomatino

**Prep Time: 10 min.**

**Cooking Time: 20 min.**

**Number of Servings: 4**

**SMARTPOINTS PER SERVING: 2**

**Ingredients**:

2 cup minced onion

1 cup minced carrot

2 medium clove, minced garlic clove

1 pound ground turkey breast, uncooked

2 ½ teaspoon Italian seasoning

1 pinch red pepper flakes

1 teaspoon kosher salt or to taste

¾ cups low-sodium chicken broth

24 ounce canned tomato puree

1 teaspoon balsamic vinegar

1 tablespoon fat-free Greek yogurt

1 tablespoon basil chopped or chopped fresh parsley

**Directions**:

1. In a cooking pot or deep saucepan, heat the oil over medium heat setting.
2. Sauté the onions until it becomes softened and translucent.
3. Mix in the garlic, hot pepper flakes turkey, carrot, Italian seasoning, and salt; stir-cook for 4-5 minutes.
4. Add the broth; stir-cook until the turkey is cooked to satisfaction.
5. Add the pureed tomato; allow to simmer for about 10-12 minutes over the low stove flame.
6. Mix in the vinegar and yogurt; season to taste.
7. Serve topped with the parsley or basil.

**Nutritional Values (Per Serving):**

Calories: 342
Fat: 4g
Saturated Fat: 0.5g
Trans Fat: 0g
Carbohydrates: 28g
Fiber: 6g
Sodium: 652mg
Protein: 34g

# Honeyed Chicken Crisp

**Prep Time:** 10 min.

**Cooking Time:** 15-20 min.

**Number of Servings:** 4

**SMARTPOINTS PER SERVING: 3**

**Ingredients:**

2 tablespoons cornstarch

½ teaspoon paprika

½ teaspoon garlic powder

4 (6-7 ounce) chicken breast fillet, pounded

¾ cups panko breadcrumbs

1 teaspoon hot sauce

Juice of 1 lemon

Ground black pepper and salt to taste

4 tablespoons oil

¼ cup honey

**Directions:**

1. Season the chicken with ground black pepper and salt to taste.
2. In a mixing bowl (medium-large size), add the breadcrumbs, paprika, garlic, and cornstarch. Combine well.
3. Coat the chicken with the mixture evenly.
4. In a saucepan or skillet, heat the oil over medium heat setting.
5. Add the coated chicken and stir cook for 6-7 minutes on each side until browned. Set aside.
6. In the pan, add the hot sauce, lemon, and honey. Combine and boil the mixture.
7. Add the chicken back and coat evenly. Serve warm.

**Nutritional Values (Per Serving):**

Calories: 419
Fat: 19g
Saturated Fat: 2.5g
Trans Fat: 0g
Carbohydrates: 33g
Fiber: 1.5g
Sodium: 201mg
Protein: 39.5g

# Vegetable Chicken with Brown Rice

**Prep Time:** 10 min.

**Cooking Time:** 10 min.

**Number of Servings:** 5-6

**SMARTPOINTS PER SERVING: 7**

**Ingredients:**

1 small zucchini, halved vertically and sliced thinly

1 red bell pepper, minced

1 chicken breast fillet, cubed

1 green pepper sliced

2 cups cooked brown rice

4 olives, pitted and chopped

1 garlic clove, minced

1 tablespoon dark or mushroom soy sauce

Zest and juice of 1 lemon

1 tablespoon apple cider vinegar

Ground black pepper and salt to taste

**Directions:**

1. In a saucepan or skillet, heat the oil over medium heat setting.
2. Add the chicken and stir-cook to evenly brown on both sides for 2-3 minutes per side.
3. Sauté the garlic and vegetables until it becomes softened and translucent for 3-4 minutes.
4. Add the soy sauce and stir-fry for 1 minute. Take it off heat.
5. Add the mixture to a bowl and add the rest of the ingredients. Toss well.
6. Serve warm.

**Nutritional Values (Per Serving):**

Calories: 171
Fat: 4g
Saturated Fat: 0.5g
Trans Fat: 0g
Carbohydrates: 38g
Fiber: 4g
Sodium: 117mg
Protein: 12g

# Potato Chicken Roast

**Prep Time:** 8-10 min.

**Cooking Time:** 20 min.

**Number of Servings:** 5-6

**SMARTPOINTS PER SERVING: 5**

**Ingredients:**

- 2 cloves garlic, minced
- 2 teaspoons fresh thyme
- 1 teaspoon black pepper
- 1 large roasting chicken
- 2 teaspoons extra-virgin olive oil
- 1 teaspoon paprika
- 1 cup baby carrots
- 1 ½ cup water
- 1 teaspoon sea salt
- 2 stalks celery, chopped
- 2 medium potatoes, cubed

**Directions:**

1. Coat the chicken with the olive oil, garlic, thyme, black pepper, paprika, and salt. Add the celery and carrots inside the chicken cavity.
2. Take an Instant Pot; open the top lid.
3. Add the chicken and water in the cooking pot. Add the potatoes.
4. Close the top lid and make sure the valve is sealed.
5. Press "MANUAL" cooking function. Adjust cooking time to 20 minutes.
6. Allow pressure to build and cook the ingredients for the set time.
7. After the set cooking time ends, press "CANCEL" and then press "NPR". Instant Pot will slowly and naturally release the pressure for 8-10 minutes.
8. Open the top lid, add the cooked mixture in serving plates. Cook on sauté for a few minutes, if you want to thicken the sauce.
9. Serve warm.

**Nutritional Values (Per Serving):**

Calories – 276

Fat – 2.5g

Carbohydrates – 12g

Fiber – 1g

Sodium - 358mg

Protein – 23.5g

# Coconut Curry Chicken

**Prep Time:** 8-10 min.

**Cooking Time:** 10 min.

**Number of Servings:** 5-6

**SMARTPOINTS PER SERVING: 7**

**Ingredients**:

- 1 tablespoon curry powder
- 1 teaspoon turmeric
- 1/4 cup lemon juice
- 1 can full-fat coconut milk
- 1/2 teaspoon lemon zest
- 1/2 teaspoon salt
- 4-pounds chicken breast, skin removed

**Directions**:

1. In a mixing bowl, mix the lemon juice, coconut milk, curry powder, turmeric, lemon zest, and salt.
2. Take an Instant Pot; open the top lid.
3. Add the chicken and bowl mix in the cooking pot. Using a spatula, gently stir to combine well.
4. Close the top lid and make sure the valve is sealed.
5. Press "POULTRY" cooking function with default cooking time.
6. Allow pressure to build and cook the ingredients for the set time.
7. After the set cooking time ends, press "CANCEL" and then press "NPR". Instant Pot will slowly and naturally release the pressure for 8-10 minutes.
8. Open the top lid, add the cooked mixture in serving plates.
9. Serve warm.

**Nutritional Values (Per Serving):**

Calories – 133

Fat – 11g

Carbohydrates – 8g

Fiber – 1.5g

Sodium - 295mg

Protein – 6.5g

# Garlic Salsa Chicken

**Prep Time:** 8-10 min.

**Cooking Time:** 25 min.

**Number of Servings:** 5-6

**SMARTPOINTS PER SERVING: 0**

**Ingredients:**

- 1/8 teaspoon oregano
- Salt as needed
- ¼ teaspoon garlic powder
- 1 ½ pound skinless chicken tenders
- 1/8 teaspoon ground cumin
- 16 ounces roasted salsa verde

**Directions:**

1. Mix the oregano, garlic powder, salt, and cumin in a mixing bowl.
2. Coat the chicken with the prepared mix and set aside for 30 minutes to season.
3. Take an Instant Pot; open the top lid.
4. Add the seasoned chicken and salsa in the cooking pot. Using a spatula, gently stir to combine well.
5. Close the top lid and make sure the valve is sealed.
6. Press "MANUAL" cooking function. Adjust cooking time to 18-20 minutes.
7. Allow pressure to build and cook the ingredients for the set time.
8. After the set cooking time ends, press "CANCEL" and then press "QPR". Instant Pot will quickly release pressure.
9. Open the top lid, shred the chicken; add the cooked mixture in serving plates.
10. Serve warm.

**Nutritional Values (Per Serving):**

Calories – 153

Fat – 2.5g

Carbohydrates – 6g

# Mexican Bean Chicken

**Prep Time:** 8-10 min.

**Cooking Time:** 25-30 min.

**Number of Servings:** 4

**SMARTPOINTS PER SERVING: 6**

**Ingredients:**

- 1 teaspoon garlic powder
- ½ teaspoon paprika
- 2 teaspoons chili powder
- 1 teaspoon cumin
- ¼ teaspoon black pepper
- ¼ teaspoon salt
- 1 green pepper, make slices
- 1 red pepper, make slices
- 1 tablespoon olive oil
- 1 pound boneless and skinless chicken breasts, make slices
- ½ onion, make slices
- 2 cups tomatoes, chopped
- 1 can black beans, rinsed and drained
- 1 cup white rice
- 1 ½ cups chicken broth

**Directions:**

1. Take a mixing bowl (either medium or large size), add in the chili powder, cumin, garlic powder, oregano, paprika, black pepper, and salt in the bowl to mix well with each other.
2. Take a skillet or saucepan (medium size preferable); heat it over a medium cooking flame.
3. Add the chicken and half of the spice mix; heat it.
4. Cook to evenly brown the chicken; add the remaining ingredients and season with the remaining spice mix.
5. Cover it. Let the mix simmer for about 25 minutes or until the rice cooks well.
6. Serve warm.

**Nutritional Values (Per Serving):**

**Calories – 523**

**Fat – 11g**

**Saturated Fats – 1g**

**Trans Fats - 0g**

**Carbohydrates – 32g**

**Fiber – 12g**

**Sodium – 623mg**

**Protein – 42g**

CHAPTER 5: PORK, BEEF & LAMB

## Classic Rosemary Roast

**Prep Time: 10-15 min.**

**Cooking Time: 75-80 min.**

**Number of Servings: 8-10**

**SMARTPOINTS PER SERVING: 3**

**Ingredients**:

3-4 cloves garlic, sliced

2-3 pound roast or eye round, fat trimmed

2 teaspoons dried chopped rosemary

Kosher salt and ground black pepper to taste

**Directions**:

1. Take the roast and make slices over the surface to make holes. Insert garlic cloves in them.
2. Lightly coat the roast with olive oil. Season to taste with salt, rosemary, and ground black pepper.
3. Preheat an oven to 350°F.
4. Grease a roasting pan or baking pan with some cooking oil.
5. Bake until the food thermometer reaches 150° F.
6. Slice thinly and serve.

**Nutritional Values (Per Serving):**

Calories: 153
Fat: 5g
Saturated Fat: 1g
Trans Fat: 0g
Carbohydrates: 3g
Fiber: 0.5g
Sodium: 301mg
Protein: 25g

# Honeyed Beef Tenderloin

**Prep Time:** 10 min.

**Cooking Time:** 10-12 min.

**Number of Servings:** 4

**SMARTPOINTS PER SERVING: 6**

**Ingredients**:

10 ounce beef tenderloin, sliced

½ head garlic, minced

¼ cup dark soy sauce

¼ cup lemon juice

1 red bell pepper

1 green bell pepper

1 red onion, sliced

2 cloves garlic, chopped

½ pear, peeled and grated

2 tablespoons honey

1 medium peeled carrots, julienned

1 bunch scallions, cut into 2-inch long

2 tablespoons olive oil

Ground black pepper and salt to taste

**Directions**:

1. In a mixing bowl, combine the beef, lemon juice, soy sauce, and garlic head.
2. Add the pear and combine it well. Set aside for 3-4 hours.
3. In a saucepan or skillet, heat the oil over medium heat setting.
4. Sauté the onions, garlic until it becomes softened and translucent.
5. Add the beef from the marinade, bell peppers, honey, and marinade mixture.
6. Season with salt, and black pepper.

7. Slowly boil the mixture; cover and allow to simmer for about 5 minutes over the low stove flame.
8. Serve warm.

**Nutritional Values (Per Serving):**

Calories: 279
Fat: 14g
Saturated Fat: 3.5g
Trans Fat: 0g
Carbohydrates: 27g
Fiber: 4g
Sodium: 183mg
Protein: 19g

## Asian Style Pork Veggies

**Prep Time:** 10 min.

**Cooking Time:** 6-10 min.

**Number of Servings:** 7-8

**SMARTPOINTS PER SERVING: 5**

**Ingredients**:

1 cup chicken stock

1 small head cabbage, chopped

1 red bell pepper, julienned

10 ounce pork tenderloin, cut into ½ inch strips

2 tablespoons cornstarch

5-6 whole corn cobs, cut into 3-4 pieces

1 small head cauliflower, cut into florets

8-10 hardboiled eggs, halved

1 medium carrots, cut into rounds

½ cup snow peas, cut in half

1 medium onion, sliced

2 cloves garlic

2 tablespoons olive oil

½ tablespoon cornstarch mixed with 2 tablespoons soy sauce

2 tablespoons oyster sauce or fish sauce

Salt and ground black pepper to taste

**Directions**:

1. In a cooking pot or deep saucepan, heat the oil over medium heat setting.
2. Sauté the onions until it becomes softened and translucent.

3. Add the garlic and cook for 1 minute.
4. Add the pork. Season with ground black pepper and salt to taste and stir the mixture.
5. Add the oyster sauce and stock; stir the mixture.
6. Add the cauliflower florets and carrots; cover and cook for 2-3 minutes.
7. Add other veggies and soy sauce mixture. Stir and cook for 2 minutes.
8. Add the eggs and stir again. Cook until the eggs are settled. Serve warm.

**Nutritional Values (Per Serving):**

Calories: 308
Fat: 11g
Saturated Fat: 3g
Trans Fat: 0g
Carbohydrates: 31g
Fiber: 7.5g
Sodium: 325mg
Protein: 20g

# Beef Stuffed Zucchini

**Prep Time:** 10 min.

**Cooking Time:** 25-30 min.

**Number of Servings:** 8

**SMARTPOINTS PER SERVING: 7**

**Ingredients:**

½ cup mozzarella cheese

½ cup cheddar cheese

4 medium zucchini, split lengthwise

10 ounce beef

2 medium tomatoes, peeled and pureed

Ground black pepper and salt to taste

1 clove garlic, minced

1 small onion, diced

**Directions:**

1. Preheat an oven to 400°F. Grease a baking pan with some cooking oil.
2. Hollow out the zucchini halves and set aside. Chop the zucchini hollowed out the flesh and set aside.
3. In a saucepan or skillet, heat the oil over medium heat setting.
4. Sauté the onions until it becomes softened and translucent. Add the garlic and cook for 1 minute.
5. Add the ground beef and stir well. Season with ground black pepper and salt to taste.
6. Add the pureed tomatoes and zucchini flesh; stir cook for 6-7 minutes. Add half portion cheese and cook until it melts completely.
7. Stuff the mixture in the zucchini halves. Arrange over prepared baking dish and top with the remaining cheeses.
8. Bake for 15 minutes or until the cheese melts. Serve warm.

**Nutritional Values (Per Serving):**

Calories: 179
Fat: 13g
Saturated Fat: 5g
Trans Fat: 0g
Carbohydrates: 9g
Fiber: 2g
Sodium: 473mg
Protein: 9g

# Beef Burger Patties

**Prep Time:** 10 min.

**Cooking Time:** 5-10 min.

**Number of Servings:** 8 (2 patties per serving)

**SMARTPOINTS PER SERVING: 5**

**Ingredients:**

10 ounce extra firm tofu, crumbled

½ teaspoon garlic powder

2 tablespoon cornstarch

2 eggs

3 leeks, white part only, minced

10 ounce beef, ground 70%

Olive oil as needed

Ground black pepper and salt to taste

**Directions:**

1. Combine the leeks and beef in a bowl. Add the garlic powder. Season with ground black pepper and salt to taste.
2. Combine well. Add the tofu and combine again.
3. Mix one egg and cornstarch. Combine well and form into 16 balls. Flatten to prepare patties.
4. In a bowl, beat the remaining egg and brush the patties with it.
5. In a saucepan or skillet, heat the oil over medium heat setting.
6. Add the patties (in batches) and stir-cook on each side to evenly brown. Serve warm.

**Nutritional Values (Per Serving):**

Calories: 264
Fat: 14g
Saturated Fat: 4g
Trans Fat: 0g
Carbohydrates: 16.5g
Fiber: 2g
Sodium: 483mg
Protein: 11g

# Zucchini Chili Beef

**Prep Time:** 8-10 min.

**Cooking Time:** 20 min.

**Number of Servings:** 4

**SMARTPOINTS PER SERVING: 6**

**Ingredients**:

- 3 minced garlic cloves
- 1 pound lean ground beef
- 1 teaspoon olive oil
- 1 chopped onion
- 1 can (4 ounce) green chilies
- 1 lime, juiced
- 1 tablespoon chili powder
- 1 can (14 ounce) tomatoes, diced
- 1 can (14 ounce) black beans, drained
- 2 chopped zucchinis
- Ground black pepper & salt as per taste

**Directions**:

1. Take a skillet or saucepan (medium size preferable); heat it over a medium cooking flame.
2. Add the oil and heat it.
3. Add the onions and garlic. Sauté for 2-3 minutes to make them soft and add the beef.
4. Cook until turns even brown; stir in the chilies, beans, tomatoes, lime juice, chili powder, pepper, and salt.
5. Continue cooking for 8-10 minutes; add the zucchini. Cook 8-10 more minutes and serve warm.

**Nutritional Values (Per Serving):**

**Calories – 374**

**Fat – 14g**

**Saturated Fats – 5g**

**Trans Fats - 0g**

**Carbohydrates – 27g**

**Fiber – 10g**

**Sodium – 237mg**

**Protein – 31g**

## Beef Burger Patties

**Prep Time: 10 min.**

**Cooking Time: 5-10 min.**

**Number of Servings: 8 (2 patties per serving)**

**SMARTPOINTS PER SERVING: 5**

**Ingredients**:

10 ounce extra firm tofu, crumbled

½ teaspoon garlic powder

2 tablespoon cornstarch

2 eggs

3 leeks, white part only, minced

10 ounce beef, ground 70%

Olive oil as needed

Ground black pepper and salt to taste

**Directions**:

7. Combine the leeks and beef in a bowl. Add the garlic powder. Season with ground black pepper and salt to taste.
8. Combine well. Add the tofu and combine again.
9. Mix one egg and cornstarch. Combine well and form into 16 balls. Flatten to prepare patties.
10. In a bowl, beat the remaining egg and brush the patties with it.
11. In a saucepan or skillet, heat the oil over medium heat setting.
12. Add the patties (in batches) and stir-cook on each side to evenly brown. Serve warm.

**Nutritional Values (Per Serving):**

Calories: 264
Fat: 14g
Saturated Fat: 4g
Trans Fat: 0g
Carbohydrates: 16.5g
Fiber: 2g
Sodium: 483mg
Protein: 11g

# Beef Parmesan Noodles

**Prep Time:** 10 min.

**Cooking Time:** 15 min.

**Number of Servings:** 3-4

**SMARTPOINTS PER SERVING: 6**

**Ingredients:**

3 cups peeled ripe tomatoes

9-10 ounce lean ground beef, fat trimmed

1 cup buckwheat noodles

1 cup beef or chicken stock

1 small red onion, chopped

2 tablespoons olive oil

Ground black pepper and salt to taste

2 garlic cloves, minced

1 tablespoon Italian seasoning

¼ cup grated parmesan cheese

**Directions:**

1. Puree the tomatoes and set aside.
2. In a saucepan or skillet, heat the oil over medium heat setting.
3. Sauté the onions until it becomes softened and translucent.
4. Add the garlic and cook for 1 minute. Add the ground beef and tomatoes.
5. Add the tomato puree and cook for about 6-7 minutes. Add the stock and bring to a boil. Season with the seasoning, salt, and ground black pepper.
6. Add the noodles and stir-cook for 3 minutes.
7. Serve warm sprinkle with grated cheese.

**Nutritional Values (Per Serving):**

Calories: 259
Fat: 13g
Saturated Fat: 3g
Trans Fat: 0g
Carbohydrates: 19g
Fiber: 2g
Sodium: 193mg
Protein: 17g

## Slow Baked Beef Vegetables

**Prep Time:** 10-15 min.

**Cooking Time:** 6 hours

**Number of Servings:** 8

**SMARTPOINTS PER SERVING: 7**

**Ingredients:**

¼ cup beef broth

1 teaspoon onion powder

36 ounce beef, roast beef cut

1 ½ cup cream of mushroom soup

2 large carrots, cut into large cubes

2 large potatoes, cut into large cubes

Ground black pepper and salt to taste

**Directions:**

1. Preheat an oven to 300°F.
2. Grease a large baking pan with some cooking oil.
3. Add all the ingredients and bake for 6 hours or until the beef is cooked well.
4. Serve warm.

**Nutritional Values (Per Serving):**

Calories: 287
Fat: 15g
Saturated Fat: 5g
Trans Fat: 0g
Carbohydrates: 16g
Fiber: 3g
Sodium: 338mg
Protein: 27g

# Baked Mustard Pork Chops

**Prep Time: 10-15 min.**

**Cooking Time: 25 min.**

**Number of Servings: 6**

**SMARTPOINTS PER SERVING: 6**

**Ingredients**:

2 tablespoons Dijon mustard

3 tablespoons bread crumbs

6 boneless and skinless pork chops, fats trimmed

1 tablespoon olive oil

Ground black pepper and salt to taste

**Directions**:

1. In a saucepan or skillet, heat the oil over medium heat setting.
2. Add the pork chops and stir-cook for 4-5 minutes on each side to evenly brown.
3. Season the pork chops to taste with salt and ground black pepper.
4. Arrange the pork chop in foil paper and add the mustard on top.
5. Add the breadcrumbs on top.
6. Preheat an oven to $300^0$F. Bake for 25 minutes and serve warm.

**Nutritional Values (Per Serving):**

Calories: 217
Fat: 9g
Saturated Fat: 2g
Trans Fat: 0g
Carbohydrates: 13g
Fiber: 2g
Sodium: 345mg
Protein: 16g

## Beef Lettuce Burgers

**Prep Time:** 8-10 min.

**Cooking Time:** 10 min.

**Number of Servings:** 4

**SMARTPOINTS PER SERVING: 4**

**Ingredients:**

- ½ teaspoon salt
- 1 tablespoon Worcestershire sauce
- 2 teaspoons garlic, minced
- ¼ teaspoon pepper
- 4 hamburger buns, low calorie
- 1 pound ground beef
- Shredded lettuce as needed

**Directions:**

1. Coat a griddle with some olive oil or cooking spray and heat it.
2. Take a mixing bowl (either medium or large size), add in the pepper, salt, Worcestershire sauce, garlic, and beef in the bowl to mix well with each other.
3. Prepare 4 patties from the mix.
4. Place them over the griddle and cook for 4-5 minutes on each side.
5. Take the buns and make burgers with your favorite toppings, lettuce, and serve.

**Nutritional Values (Per Serving):**

**Calories – 327**

**Fat – 12g**

**Saturated Fats – 5g**

**Trans Fats - 0g**

**Carbohydrates – 22g**

**Fiber – 1g**

**Sodium – 642mg**

**Protein – 27g**

## Creamy Pork Chops

**Prep Time:** 8-10 min.

**Cooking Time:** 15 min.

**Number of Servings:** 4

**SMARTPOINTS PER SERVING: 5**

**Ingredients:**

- 4 pork loin chops, center-cut
- 1/3 cup non-fat, half-and-half
- 1/3 cup fat-free chicken stock
- 1/2 teaspoon salt
- 1 1/2 tablespoon Dijon mustard
- 1/2 teaspoon black pepper
- 1/2 teaspoon onion powder
- Pinch of dried thyme

**Directions:**

1. Rub the salt, pepper, and onion powder over the chops.
2. Take a skillet or saucepan (medium size preferable); heat it over a medium cooking flame.
3. Add the oil and heat it.
4. Add the meat and cook, while stirring, until turns evenly brown for 3-4 minute per side.
5. Pour the stock, mustard, and half-and-half.
6. Lower temperature setting; cook for 6-7 more minutes.
7. When the sauce becomes thick, add the thyme. Serve warm.

**Nutritional Values (Per Serving):**

**Calories – 134**

**Fat – 5g**

**Saturated Fats – 2g**

**Trans Fats - 0g**

**Carbohydrates – 2g**

**Fiber – 0g**

**Sodium – 447mg**

**Protein – 14g**

# Beef Broccoli Dinner

**Prep Time:** 8-10 min.

**Cooking Time:** 10-15 min.

**Number of Servings:** 4

**SMARTPOINTS PER SERVING: 3**

**Ingredients**:

- 3/4 pound lean sirloin beef
- 1/4 teaspoon salt
- 5 cups broccoli florets
- 1 cup chicken broth, reduced-sodium
- 2 ½ tablespoon cornstarch
- 2 teaspoon canola oil
- 1/4 cup water
- 1/4 teaspoon red pepper flakes
- 2 tablespoon minced garlic
- 1/4 cup soy sauce
- 1 tablespoon minced ginger root

**Directions**:

1. Combine the 2 tablespoons cornstarch and salt; coat the beef with it.
2. Take a skillet or saucepan (medium size preferable); heat it over a medium cooking flame.
3. Add the oil and heat it.
4. Add the beef and cook, while stirring, until turns evenly brown for 3-4 minutes. Set the beef aside.
5. Add ½ cup of the broth, broccoli and cook for 2-3 minutes.
6. Add the garlic, ginger, and pepper flakes. Simmer the mix for 1 more minute.
7. Take a mixing bowl (either medium or large size), add in the rest of the broth, soy sauce, and rest of the cornstarch in the bowl to mix well with each other.
8. Turn down heat; cover and simmer for 1 minute. Mix in the broth mix and beef; serve warm.

**Nutritional Values (Per Serving):**

**Calories – 253**

**Fat – 11g**

**Saturated Fats – 3g**

**Trans Fats - 0g**

**Carbohydrates – 7g**

**Fiber – 1g**

**Sodium – 753mg**

**Protein – 27g**

# Roast Taco Wraps

**Prep Time: 8-10 min.**

**Cooking Time: 0 min.**

**Number of Servings: 7**

**SMARTPOINTS PER SERVING: 6**

**Ingredients:**

- ½ pound cooked roast beef, make slices
- 2 make slices tomatoes
- ¼ teaspoon pepper
- 7 pieces tortilla
- 2 teaspoon Dijon mustard
- 1/3 cup basil
- 1/3 cup mayo
- 2 cup shredded lettuce
- ¼ teaspoon salt

**Directions:**

1. Take a mixing bowl (either medium or large size), add in the pepper, mustard, salt, basil, and mayo in the bowl to mix well with each other.
2. Arrange the tortillas and spread the mix; top with some lettuce, roast beef, and tomatoes. Roll the tortillas and serve.

**Nutritional Values (Per Serving):**

**Calories – 193**

**Fat – 9g**

**Saturated Fats – 2g**

**Trans Fats - 0g**

**Carbohydrates – 16g**

**Fiber – 1g**

**Sodium – 647mg**

**Protein – 12g**

## Grilled Spiced Chops

**Prep Time:** 8-10 min.

**Cooking Time:** 8 min.

**Number of Servings:** 4

**SMARTPOINTS PER SERVING: 6**

**Ingredients:**

- 2 teaspoons brown sugar
- 1 1/3 pound boneless pork chops
- 2 teaspoons vegetable oil
- 2 teaspoons sweet paprika
- 1/2 teaspoon ground garlic powder
- 1/2 teaspoon ground cinnamon
- 1/2 teaspoon kosher salt
- 1/2 teaspoon ground ginger

**Directions:**

1. Take a mixing bowl (either medium or large size), add in the paprika, sugar, chili powder, cinnamon, salt, ginger, and garlic powder in the bowl to mix well with each other.
2. Rub over the chops.
3. Preheat your grill over medium-high temperature setting.
4. Grill 3-4 minutes for each side; until cooks well.
5. Serve warm.

**Nutritional Values (Per Serving):**

**Calories – 367**

**Fat – 23g**

**Saturated Fats – 3g**

**Trans Fats - 0g**

**Carbohydrates – 3g**

**Fiber – 0g**

**Sodium – 283mg**

**Protein – 36g**

CHAPTER 6: FISH & SEAFOOD

## Baked Herbed Salmon

**Prep Time:** 10 min.

**Cooking Time:** 15-20 min.

**Number of Servings:** 4

**SMARTPOINTS PER SERVING: 1**

**Ingredients**:

4 (6 ounce each) salmon fillets

2 tarragon sprigs

4 garlic cloves minced

4 slices large tomatoes, seeded

2 fennel sprigs

4 teaspoon butter

¼ cup wine

Ground black pepper and salt to taste

**Directions**:

1. Season the salmon with ground black pepper and salt to taste. Set aside.
2. In a mixing bowl (medium-large size), add the garlic and wine. Combine well.
3. Preheat an oven to 350°F. Grease a baking pan with some cooking oil.
4. Add the salmon in the baking pan and add the butter on top; top with the tomato slices, fennel, and tarragon sprigs.
5. Add the garlic and wine mixture on top.
6. Bake for 15-20 minutes; serve warm.

**Nutritional Values (Per Serving):**

Calories: 403
Fat: 18g
Saturated Fat: 2g
Trans Fat: 0g
Carbohydrates: 14g
Fiber: 2g
Sodium: 183mg
Protein: 38g

# Creamed Halibut

**Prep Time: 10 min.**

**Cooking Time: 15 min.**

**Number of Servings: 4**

**SMARTPOINTS PER SERVING: 3**

**Ingredients**:

2 tablespoons butter

¼ cup heavy cream

6 cups fish stock

4 (6 ounce) halibut steak

1 tablespoon each of parsley and thyme

3 tablespoons flour

Salt, ground black pepper and paprika to taste

**Directions**:

1. In a saucepan or skillet, heat the stock over medium heat setting.
2. Add the halibut and boil the mixture. Allow simmering for about 12 minutes over the low stove flame.
3. Season with ground black pepper and salt to taste. Turn off the heat.
4. Take out the fish and arrange on a serving plate. Also, take out 1 ½ cups of the fish stock.
5. In a saucepan or skillet, heat the butter over medium heat setting.
6. Add the flour and stir well. Add the fish stock and boil the mixture.
7. Add the cream; stir cook for 1 minute. Season with paprika, salt, and pepper.
8. Add the mixture over the prepared steaks. Serve topped with the parsley and thyme.

**Nutritional Values (Per Serving):**

Calories: 568
Fat: 31g
Saturated Fat: 14g
Trans Fat: 0g
Carbohydrates: 8g
Fiber: 0.5g
Sodium: 814mg
Protein: 47g

# Classic Crab Cakes

**Prep Time: 10-15 min.**

**Cooking Time: 30 min.**

**Number of Servings: 8**

**SMARTPOINTS PER SERVING: 3**

**Ingredients**:

2 egg whites, beaten

1 whole egg, beaten

16 ounce crab meat

1 cup corn kernels

1 cup crackers, crushed

1/4 cup red bell pepper, minced

4 scallions, chopped fine

2 tablespoons yogurt, fat-free

2 tablespoons mayonnaise

1/4 cup parsley

Juice of 1 lemon

Ground black pepper and salt to taste to taste

**Directions**:

1. In a mixing bowl (medium-large size), add the scallions, crackers, corn, eggs, black pepper, parsley, lemon juice, mayo, yogurt, ground black pepper, and salt. Combine well.
2. Add the crab meat and combine the mixture. Prepare 8 patties from the mixture and refrigerate for 1 hour.
3. Preheat an oven to 425°F. Grease a baking sheet with some cooking oil.
4. Bake about 25 minutes or until golden brown. Serve warm.

**Nutritional Values (Per Serving):**

Calories: 103

Fat: 3g
Saturated Fat: 0.5g
Trans Fat: 0g
Carbohydrates: 8g
Fiber: 1g
Sodium: 376mg
Protein: 11.5g

## Classic Ginger Garlic Fish

**Prep Time:** 10 min.

**Cooking Time:** 20-25 min.

**Number of Servings:** 4

**SMARTPOINTS PER SERVING: 1**

**Ingredients**:

3 cloves garlic, minced

2/3 cups water

4 medium whole fish (cod, salmon etc.)

1 teaspoon sugar

Pinch of ground black pepper and salt to taste

1 tablespoon olive oil

1 thumb size ginger, peeled and sliced

1 large red onion, sliced

3 tablespoons fish sauce

¼ cup vinegar

**Directions**:

1. Heat a saucepan or skillet over the medium stove flame.
2. Add all the ingredients except for the fish and olive oil.
3. Boil without stirring and add the fish and oil; stir the mixture.
4. Cover and allow to simmer for about 15 minutes over low stove flame until the fish is easy to flake.
5. Serve warm.

**Nutritional Values (Per Serving):**

Calories: 125
Fat: 4g
Saturated Fat: 1g
Trans Fat: 0g
Carbohydrates: 7g
Fiber: 0g
Sodium: 536mg
Protein: 5g

# Tuna Mayonnaise Sandwich

**Prep Time:** 10-15 min.

**Cooking Time:** 1 min.

**Number of Servings:** 2

**SMARTPOINTS PER SERVING: 2**

**Ingredients:**

1 tablespoon butter

1 teaspoon dill, minced

½ cup flaked tuna in water

1 teaspoon mayonnaise

Dash of cayenne pepper

1 hardboiled egg, grated

4 rye or whole wheat bread slices

Ground black pepper and salt to taste

**Directions:**

1. In a mixing bowl (medium-large size), add the tuna, egg, mayonnaise, dill, cayenne, salt, and pepper.
2. Combine well.
3. Take the bread slices; brush with butter on both sides. Grill them in the saucepan to evenly brown.
4. Arrange the tuna mixture and serve fresh.

**Nutritional Values (Per Serving):**

Calories: 429
Fat: 13g
Saturated Fat: 5g
Trans Fat: 0g
Carbohydrates: 43g
Fiber: 6g
Sodium: 416mg
Protein: 26g

**Saucy Carrot Shrimp**

**Prep Time:** 10 min.

**Cooking Time:** 15 min.

**Number of Servings:** 4

**SMARTPOINTS PER SERVING: 2**

**Ingredients**:

2 cloves garlic

1 teaspoon ginger, minced

17-18 ounce large shrimps, peeled and deveined

1 large white onion, sliced thinly

1 small carrot, julienned

¼ cup tomato ketchup

1 green pepper

1 red pepper

3 tablespoons brown sugar

2 tablespoons spring onions chopped

1 tablespoon fish sauce

¼ cup vinegar

1 teaspoon chili powder, optional

Ground black pepper and salt to taste

Olive oil

**Directions**:

1. In a cooking pot or deep saucepan, heat 4 tablespoons oil over medium heat setting.
2. Add the shrimp and stir cook for 5 minutes. Add the carrots and season with ground black pepper and salt to taste.

3. Stir-cook for another 2 minutes. Set aside the mixture.
4. In the pan, sauté the red onion with some cooking oil. Add the sugar and combine to melt.
5. Add the vinegar and boil the mixture. Add the ginger and garlic; stir cook for 1 minute.
6. Add the ketchup, chili powder, and the fish sauce. Add the shrimp mixture and coat well.
7. Serve with the spring onions on top.

**Nutritional Values (Per Serving):**

Calories: 386
Fat: 15g
Saturated Fat: 1g
Trans Fat: 0g
Carbohydrates: 33g
Fiber: 7g
Sodium: 1024mg
Protein: 36g

# Wholesome Salmon Vegetables

**Prep Time:** 10 min.

**Cooking Time:** 15 min.

**Number of Servings:** 4

**SMARTPOINTS PER SERVING: 1**

**Ingredients:**

1 red onion, julienned

1 medium carrot, julienned

4 (6 ounce each) salmon steaks (you can use tuna steaks as well)

1 medium zucchini, julienned

1 green pepper julienned

1 red pepper julienned

½ cup dry white wine

1 tablespoon butter

Juice of 1 lemon

3 cups water

1 teaspoon parsley, chopped

Ground black pepper and salt to taste

**Directions:**

1. In a saucepan or skillet, heat the butter over medium heat setting.
2. Add the vegetables except for the onion; stir cook for 2-3 minutes. Set aside.
3. Sauté the onions until it becomes softened and translucent
4. Add the white wine and cook until reduced in quantity. Add the water and lemon juice and add the fish steaks.
5. Slowly boil the mixture; cover and allow to simmer for about 12 minutes over the low stove flame.
6. Season with Ground black pepper and salt to taste. Add back the vegetables and cook for 1 minute. Serve warm.

**Nutritional Values (Per Serving):**

Calories: 324
Fat: 23g
Saturated Fat: 7g
Trans Fat: 0g
Carbohydrates: 16g
Fiber: 3g
Sodium: 512mg
Protein: 39g

# Avocado Tuna Salad

**Prep Time: 10 min.**

**Cooking Time: 0 min.**

**Number of Servings: 4**

**SMARTPOINTS PER SERVING: 1**

**Ingredients**:

2 tablespoons apple cider vinegar

1 teaspoon olive oil

2 (6 ounce each) grilled tuna, flaked

¼ cup avocado

2 stalks scallions, minced

2 stalks celery, chopped

Ground black pepper and salt to taste

**Directions**:

1. In a mixing bowl, mash the avocado and vinegar. Season with ground black pepper and salt to taste.
2. Add the flaked tuna and mix well.
3. In another mixing bowl, combine the scallions, olive oil, and celery.
4. Add to the tuna mixture and combine. Serve fresh!

**Nutritional Values (Per Serving):**

Calories: 106
Fat: 5g
Saturated Fat: 0g
Trans Fat: 0g
Carbohydrates: 11g
Fiber: 1g
Sodium: 157mg
Protein: 6g

# Herbed Seafood Meal

**Prep Time: 10-15 min.**

**Cooking Time: 5 min.**

**Number of Servings: 3-4**

**SMARTPOINTS PER SERVING: 3**

**Ingredients**:

14 ounce large shrimp, peeled and deveined

3 tablespoons cornstarch

14 ounce cod or any white fish fillet, thinly sliced

1 teaspoon wild chives, minced

¼ cup canola oil

Ground black pepper and salt to taste

2 large eggs

**Directions**:

1. Season the fish slices with ground black pepper and salt to taste.
2. Butterfly the shrimps using a knife. Season with ground black pepper and salt to taste. Beat the 2 eggs in a bowl. Add the cornstarch and combine it well. Add the chives and combine them again.
3. Coat the fish and shrimps with the egg mixture.
4. In a saucepan or skillet, heat the oil over medium heat setting.
5. Add the shrimps and fish; stir-cook for 2-3 minutes per side until evenly browned and cooked well.
6. Serve warm.

**Nutritional Values (Per Serving):**

Calories: 294
Fat: 16g
Saturated Fat: 2g
Trans Fat: 0g
Carbohydrates: 8g
Fiber: 0g
Sodium: 824mg
Protein: 39g

## Avocado Crab Salad

**Prep Time: 8-10 min.**

**Cooking Time: 0 min.**

**Number of Servings: 2**

**SMARTPOINTS PER SERVING: 5**

**Ingredients**:

- 2 teaspoons Asian hot sauce
- 1 teaspoon fresh chives
- 2 teaspoons low-fat mayo
- 4-ounce crabmeat, chopped
- 1/4 cup cucumber, diced

**For the Avocado:**

- 1 small ripe avocado, pitted and sliced
- 2 teaspoon soy sauce
- 1/2 teaspoon sesame seeds

**Directions**:

1. Take a mixing bowl (either medium or large size), add in the ingredients except for the soy sauce and sesame seeds in the bowl to mix well with each other.
2. Top with the sauce and seeds; serve.

**Nutritional Values (Per Serving):**

**Calories – 178**

**Fat – 12g**

**Saturated Fats – 2g**

**Trans Fats - 0g**

**Carbohydrates – 11g**

**Fiber – 5g**

**Sodium – 563mg**

**Protein – 13g**

## Potato Mayo Fish

**Prep Time:** 8-10 min.

**Cooking Time:** 12 min.

**Number of Servings:** 3

**SMARTPOINTS PER SERVING: 4**

**Ingredients:**

- ½ teaspoon lemon juice
- ½ teaspoon ground mustard
- 3 tablespoons light mayonnaise
- ½ teaspoon pickle relish
- 2 tablespoons green onions, chopped
- Pepper and salt as per taste
- ½ cup butter, melted
- 4 (3-ounce) tilapia fillet
- ½ cup potato flakes

**Directions:**

1. Preheat an oven to 450°F.
2. Take a mixing bowl (either medium or large size), add in the mayonnaise, pickle, lemon juice, mustard, and green onions in the bowl to mix well with each other.
3. Coat the fish with the mayo mixture and then dredge on the potato flakes; pat gently and sprinkle with pepper and salt as per taste.
4. Arrange over a baking sheet and bake for 12 minutes. After 6 minutes, brush with the butter and cook for 6 more minutes. Serve warm.

**Nutritional Values (Per Serving):**

**Calories – 533**

**Fat – 32g**

**Saturated Fats – 18g**

**Trans Fats - 0g**

**Carbohydrates – 6g**

**Fiber – 1g**

**Sodium – 654mg**

**Protein – 13g**

## Tuna Cranberry Salad

**Prep Time: 8-10 min.**

**Cooking Time: 0 min.**

**Number of Servings: 5**

**SMARTPOINTS PER SERVING: 3**

**Ingredients**:

**Seasoning:**

- Red pepper flakes, black pepper, sea salt as needed

**Salad:**

- 3 tablespoons light sour cream
- 1 can (16 ounce) white tuna in spring water
- 3 tables low-fat mayonnaise
- 1/4 cup red onion, minced
- 1 tablespoon lemon juice
- 1 cored apple, sliced
- 1/4 cup dried cranberries
- 1/2 cup celery, chopped

**Directions**:

1. Take a mixing bowl (either medium or large size), add in the salad ingredients in the bowl to mix well with each other.
2. Season as needed and serve.

**Nutritional Values (Per Serving):**

**Calories – 83**

**Fat – 1g**

**Saturated Fats – 0g**

**Trans Fats - 0g**

**Carbohydrates – 13g**

**Fiber – 2g**

**Sodium – 164mg**

**Protein – 4g**

# Salmon Asparagus Treat

**Prep Time:** 8-10 min.

**Cooking Time:** 15 min.

**Number of Servings:** 4

**SMARTPOINTS PER SERVING: 4**

**Ingredients:**

- 2 tablespoons lemon juice
- 1/2 teaspoon oregano
- 4 salmon fillets
- 2 tablespoons Dijon mustard
- 1/2 teaspoon dried dill
- pepper and salt as needed
- 1 pound asparagus
- 1 pound thinly sliced sweet potatoes
- 2 minced garlic cloves
- 1 tablespoon olive oil

**Directions:**

1. Preheat an oven to 450°F.
2. Take a mixing bowl (either medium or large size), add in the oregano, half of the garlic, lemon juice, dill, and mustard in the bowl to mix well with each other.
3. Arrange the fillets in the pan and brush with the sauce.
4. Combine the salt, pepper, oil, and rest of the garlic in another mixing bowl.
5. Mix in the asparagus and potato slices.
6. Arrange the vegetables in a greased baking pan and bake for 12-15 minutes until the fish is flaky.
7. Serve warm.

**Nutritional Values (Per Serving):**

**Calories – 327**

**Fat – 14g**

**Saturated Fats – 2g**

**Trans Fats - 0g**

**Carbohydrates – 23g**

**Fiber – 5g**

**Sodium – 163mg**

**Protein – 26g**

# CHAPTER 7: MEATLESS

## Kale Quinoa Salad

**Prep Time:** 10-15 min.

**Cooking Time:** 5 min.

**Number of Servings:** 4

**SMARTPOINTS PER SERVING: 7**

**Ingredients:**

Dressing:

Juice of 1 lemon

1 teaspoon maple syrup

2 tablespoons olive oil, extra-virgin

1 large garlic clove, minced

1 small shallot, minced

Ground black pepper and kosher salt to taste

**Salad:**

1 bunch kale, trimmed and chopped

¼ cup dried cranberries

1 cup quinoa, cooked

¼ cup toasted almonds, sliced

2 tablespoons Parmesan cheese, grated

**Directions:**

1. In a mixing bowl (medium-large size), add the dressing ingredients. Combine well.
2. Add the kale with the dressing. Toss well.
3. Add half the almonds, half cranberries, and quinoa; toss well.

4. Add remaining almonds and cranberries on top; serve fresh with the cheese on top.

**Nutritional Values (Per Serving):**

Calories: 226
Fat: 11g
Saturated Fat: 1.5g
Trans Fat: 0g
Carbohydrates: 27g
Fiber: 3g
Sodium: 149mg
Protein: 6g

## Egg Cheese Sandwich

**Prep Time:** 10 min.

**Cooking Time:** 6 min.

**Number of Servings:** 1

**SMARTPOINTS PER SERVING: 3**

**Ingredients**:

1 thin slice cheddar or Swiss cheese

1 egg

1 thick slice mozzarella

½ cup cabbage, shredded

1 teaspoon honey mustard

2 tablespoons flour

Ground black pepper and salt to taste

4 teaspoon butter

Olive oil

4 slices of rye or whole wheat bread

**Directions**:

1. In a mixing bowl, beat the eggs. Add the flour; combine well. Add the shredded cabbage and combine again.
2. In a saucepan or skillet, heat the oil over medium heat setting.
3. Sauté the cabbage mixture for 1-2 minutes.
4. In a non-stick pan, put a little bit of oil and pour the cabbage mixture. Cook for about a minute on each side. Set aside.
5. Melt half the butter and add two bread slices; on top, add the mozzarella cheese.
6. Add the cabbage mixture over the bread and top with the cheddar cheese.
7. Cook for about 2 minutes; arrange the other bread slices on top. Take out the bread sandwiches.
8. Melt remaining butter and place the sandwich back with non-buttered side. Cook for 1-2 minutes and serve.

**Nutritional Values (Per Serving):**

Calories: 362
Fat: 23g
Saturated Fat: 8g
Trans Fat: 0g
Carbohydrates: 19g
Fiber: 5g
Sodium: 951mg
Protein: 16g

# Squash Cheese Risotto

**Prep Time:** 10-15 min.

**Cooking Time:** 2 min.

**Number of Servings:** 8

**SMARTPOINTS PER SERVING: 3**

**Ingredients:**

1 cup squash cubes

¼ cup white wine

4 cups chicken or beef stock

1 ½ cups long grain rice

½ cup sage leaves, torn

1/3 cup Parmesan cheese

1 tablespoon olive oil

1 medium white onion

Ground black pepper and salt to taste

**Directions:**

1. In a cooking pot or deep saucepan, heat the oil over medium heat setting.
2. Sauté the onions until it becomes softened and translucent.
3. Add the squash and stir-cook for about 2 minutes.
4. Add the rice and cook for 4-5 minutes. Season with ground black pepper and salt to taste.
5. Add the white wine and chicken stock.
6. Slowly boil the mixture; cover and allow to simmer until the rice is cooked well over the low stove flame.
7. Mix in the sage leaves. Serve with the parmesan cheese on top.

**Nutritional Values (Per Serving):**

Calories: 343
Fat: 12g
Saturated Fat: 3g
Trans Fat: 0g
Carbohydrates: 42g
Fiber: 4g
Sodium: 334mg
Protein: 10g

# Broccoli Cauliflower Curry

**Prep Time:** 10-15 min.

**Cooking Time:** 10 min.

**Number of Servings:** 6-8

**SMARTPOINTS PER SERVING: 0**

**Ingredients**:

2 large potatoes, peeled and cubed

1 small carrot, diced

1 small head cauliflower, cut into florets

1 small head broccoli, cut into florets

¼ cup peas

2 cloves garlic

2 teaspoons green or red curry powder

1 large red onion, sliced

1 red bell pepper, cut in large wedges

¾ cup tomato paste

¾ cup water

1 tablespoon olive oil

**Directions**:

1. In a mixing bowl (medium-large size), add the curry powder and 1 tablespoon of water. Combine well.
2. In a saucepan or skillet, heat the oil over medium heat setting.
3. Sauté the onions until becomes softened and translucent.
4. Add the garlic and cook for 1 minute.
5. Add the curry paste; stir-cook until turn fragrant. Add the water and bring to a boil.
6. Add the vegetables and cook for 7-8 minutes or until become tender. Serve warm.

**Nutritional Values (Per Serving):**

Calories: 146
Fat: 4g
Saturated Fat: 0g
Trans Fat: 0g
Carbohydrates: 21g
Fiber: 7g
Sodium: 91mg
Protein: 6g

# Bean Red Onion Salad

**Prep Time: 10 min.**

**Cooking Time: 5 min.**

**Number of Servings: 4**

**SMARTPOINTS PER SERVING: 4**

**Ingredients**:

2 cups cooked white beans

1 garlic clove, minced

1 tablespoon parsley, minced

1 tablespoon butter

2 tablespoons white wine vinegar

1 teaspoon Dijon mustard

2 small red onions, chopped finely

5 tablespoons extra virgin olive oil

Ground black pepper and salt to taste

**Directions**:

1. In a mixing bowl (medium-large size), add the vinegar, mustard, olive oil. Combine well. Season with ground black pepper and salt to taste.
2. In a saucepan or skillet, heat the butter over medium heat setting.
3. Sauté the onions until it becomes softened and translucent.
4. Add the garlic and cook for 1 minute. Season with ground black pepper and salt to taste.
5. Add the parsley and toss.
6. Add the mixture to a bowl. Add the vinegar dressing on top and toss.
7. Serve warm.

**Nutritional Values (Per Serving):**

Calories: 322
Fat: 19g
Saturated Fat: 4g
Trans Fat: 0g
Carbohydrates: 23g
Fiber: 10g
Sodium: 442mg
Protein: 9g

# Zucchini Cheese Noodles

**Prep Time:** 15 min.

**Cooking Time:** 1 min.

**Number of Servings:** 3-4

**SMARTPOINTS PER SERVING: 2**

**Ingredients:**

1 cup mozzarella cheese, cubed

¼ cup olive oil

5 medium zucchini, spiralized into noodle shape

1-2 cups cherry tomatoes, halved

¼ cup balsamic vinegar

Ground black pepper and salt to taste

1 handful basil leaves, chopped

**Directions:**

1. Boil the zoodles in a cooking pot for 10-15 seconds. Drain and set aside. Season with ground black pepper and salt to taste.
2. In a mixing bowl, combine the vinegar and olive oil.
3. Drizzle the mixture over the zoodles. Toss well and set aside for 5 minutes.
4. Add remaining ingredients and toss. Serve fresh!

**Nutritional Values (Per Serving):**

Calories: 223
Fat: 14g
Saturated Fat: 2g
Trans Fat: 0g
Carbohydrates: 14g
Fiber: 4g
Sodium: 271mg
Protein: 11g

# Potato Buttermilk Appetizer

**Prep Time:** 8-10 min.

**Cooking Time:** 12 min.

**Number of Servings:** 6

**SMARTPOINTS PER SERVING: 4**

**Ingredients:**

- 1/3 cup buttermilk, low-fat
- ½ teaspoon kosher salt
- ¼ cup sour cream
- 3 cups water
- 2-pound russet potatoes, peeled and make quarters
- 1 teaspoon salt
- 2 tablespoons butter
- Parsley as required, chopped
- Black pepper as needed

**Directions:**

1. Take an Instant Pot; open the top lid.
2. Add the water, salt, and potato in the cooking pot. Using a spatula, gently stir to combine well.
3. Close the top lid and make sure the valve is sealed.
4. Press "MANUAL" cooking function. Adjust cooking time to 10-12 minutes.
5. Allow pressure to build and cook the ingredients for the set time.
6. After the set cooking time ends, press "CANCEL" and then press "QPR". Instant Pot will quickly release pressure.
7. Open the top lid, drain water except for ½ cup and add the potatoes in a blender. Add ½ cup of water also.
8. Add in the remaining ingredients and blend to create a mash like consistency.
9. Serve warm.

**Nutritional Values (Per Serving):**

Calories - 138

Fat – 4.5g

Carbohydrates – 26.5g

Fiber – 3g

Sodium - 312mg

Protein – 5g

## Orange Glazed Potatoes

**Prep Time:** 8-10 min.

**Cooking Time:** 20 min.

**Number of Servings:** 7-8

**SMARTPOINTS PER SERVING: 4**

**Ingredients:**

- 1 tablespoon cinnamon
- 1 tablespoon blackstrap molasses
- ½ cup orange juice
- 4 cups sweet potatoes, make small-sized pieces
- 1 teaspoon vanilla
- ¼ cup sugar

**Directions:**

1. In a heat-proof bowl, add the potatoes. Mix in the cinnamon, molasses, sugar, orange juice, and vanilla.
2. Take an Instant Pot; open the top lid.
3. Pour 1 cup water and place steamer basket/trivet inside the cooking pot.
4. Arrange the bowl over the basket/trivet.
5. Close the top lid and make sure the valve is sealed.
6. Press "MANUAL" cooking function. Adjust cooking time to 20-22 minutes.
7. Allow pressure to build and cook the ingredients for the set time.
8. After the set cooking time ends, press "CANCEL" and then press "NPR". Instant Pot will slowly and naturally release the pressure for 8-10 minutes.
9. Open the top lid, add the cooked mixture in serving plates.
10. Serve warm.

**Nutritional Values (Per Serving):**

Calories - 112

Fat – 4.5g

Carbohydrates – 16g

Fiber – 3g

Sodium - 173mg

Protein – 3g

# Broccoli Spinach Greens

**Prep Time:** 8-10 min.

**Cooking Time:** 5 min.

**Number of Servings:** 4-5

**SMARTPOINTS PER SERVING: 1**

**Ingredients:**

- 2 cups kale, chopped
- 1/2 teaspoon cumin, ground
- 2 cups broccoli, chopped
- 2 cups baby spinach
- 1/2 teaspoon coriander, ground
- 2 cloves garlic, crushed or minced
- 2 tablespoons coconut oil
- 1 tablespoon ginger, minced

**Directions:**

1. Take an Instant Pot; open the top lid.
2. Press "SAUTÉ" cooking function.
3. In the cooking pot area, add the oil, garlic, ginger, and broccoli. Cook until turn translucent and softened for 4-5 minutes.
4. Add the remaining ingredients.
5. Cook until spinach and kale are wilted.
6. Add the cooked mixture in serving plates.
7. Serve warm.

**Nutritional Values (Per Serving):**

Calories - 93

Fat – 5.5g

Carbohydrates – 4g

Fiber – 1g

Sodium - 33mg

Protein – 4.5g

# Mango Arugula Salad

**Prep Time:** 8-10 min.

**Cooking Time:** 0 min.

**Number of Servings:** 4-5

**SMARTPOINTS PER SERVING:** 3

**Ingredients:**

- 4 cups baby arugula
- 3 tablespoons chopped walnuts
- 1 tablespoon vinegar, balsamic
- 1 tablespoon olive oil, extra virgin
- 3 medium ripe mangos, seeded and make slices
- ¾ cup red onion, make slices
- 1/2 tablespoon lemon juice
- 1/8 tablespoon lemon zest
- Black pepper and salt as per taste

**Directions:**

1. Take a mixing bowl (either medium or large size), add in the peaches, yellow pepper, arugula, and walnuts in the bowl to mix well with each other.
2. In a bowl whisk the olive oil, vinegar, lemon juice, pepper and salt and drizzle over the salad. Serve fresh.

**Nutritional Values (Per Serving):**

**Calories** – 192

**Fat** – 7g

**Saturated Fats** – 1g

**Trans Fats** - 0g

**Carbohydrates** – 33g

**Fiber** – 4g

**Sodium** – 24mg

**Protein** – 3g

# Cream Mayo Corn

**Prep Time:** 8-10 min.

**Cooking Time:** 20 min.

**Number of Servings:** 8

**SMARTPOINTS PER SERVING: 2**

**Ingredients**:

- ¼ cup grated Parmesan cheese
- ½ cup Greek yogurt, plain and non-fat
- 16-ounce bag frozen sweet corn on the cob
- ½ cup fat-free mayonnaise
- ½ teaspoon cayenne pepper
- Pepper and salt as per taste

**Directions**:

1. Take a mixing bowl (either medium or large size), add in all the ingredients in the bowl to mix well with each other.
2. Preheat your grill over high-temperature setting.
3. Arrange the corn ears in a cooking pan and cover with a foil. Grill for 18-20 minutes.
4. Serve warm.

**Nutritional Values (Per Serving):**

**Calories** – 272

**Fat** – 16g

**Saturated Fats** – 9g

**Trans Fats** - 0g

**Carbohydrates** – 9g

**Fiber** – 2g

**Sodium** – 961mg

**Protein** – 22g

# CHAPTER 8: DESSERTS

## Apple Yogurt Parfait

**Prep Time:** 10-15 min.

**Cooking Time:** 2 min.

**Number of Servings:** 1

**SMARTPOINTS PER SERVING: 4**

**Ingredients:**

2 teaspoons honey

1/2 cup plain Greek yogurt

2 teaspoons cornstarch

1 cup green apples, peeled and chopped

1/4 teaspoon vanilla extract

¼ cup ground graham crackers

Pinch of salt

1/4 teaspoon cinnamon

**Directions:**

1. In a heat-proof bowl (medium-large size), add the apples, cornstarch, honey, salt, cinnamon, and vanilla. Combine well.
2. Add in the microwave and cook for 2 minutes.
3. In a glass, add half the yogurt first and top with the half apple mixture. Sprinkle with half ground crackers.
4. Repeat to make other layers. Serve warm.

**Nutritional Values (Per Serving):**

Calories: 378
Fat: 6g
Saturated Fat: 0g

Trans Fat: 0g
Carbohydrates: 36g
Fiber: 2g
Sodium: 468mg
Protein: 11g

# Cheesy Cracker Cups

**Prep Time:** 10 min.

**Cooking Time:** 0 min.

**Number of Servings:** 4

**SMARTPOINTS PER SERVING: 4**

**Ingredients:**

4 teaspoons strawberry or blueberry jam

Fresh sliced strawberry or blueberries to serve

5-6 graham crackers, ground

1 cup ricotta cheese

Evaporated milk as required

**Directions:**

1. In a mixing bowl (medium-large size), add the crackers and milk. Combine well to make a soft dough.
2. Create 4 balls from the dough.
3. At the bottom of four muffin tins, press the balls flat. Add the ricotta cheese and level it slightly.
4. Add the jam on top and arrange the slices of strawberry or blueberries. Enjoy.

**Nutritional Values (Per Serving):**

Calories: 236
Fat: 9g
Saturated Fat: 5g
Trans Fat: 0g
Carbohydrates: 27g
Fiber: 2g
Sodium: 203mg
Protein: 9g

# Cream Mango Chill

**Prep Time:** 10 min.

**Cooking Time:** 0 min.

**Number of Servings:** 1

**SMARTPOINTS PER SERVING: 3**

**Ingredients:**

¼ cup cream

¼ cup condensed milk

¼ cup evaporated milk

1 ripe mango, remove seed and flesh chopped

2 cups shaved ice

1 tablespoon sugar

Pinch of salt

**Directions:**

1. In a serving bowl, add the shaved ice; top it with the mangoes.
2. In another bowl, combine other ingredients.
3. Add over the mango and serve chilled!

**Nutritional Values (Per Serving):**

Calories: 402
Fat: 13g
Saturated Fat: 7g
Trans Fat: 0g
Carbohydrates: 38g
Fiber: 3g
Sodium: 244mg
Protein: 7g

## Blueberry Lemon Muffins

**Prep Time:** 8-10 min.

**Cooking Time:** 25 min.

**Number of Servings:** 15

**SMARTPOINTS PER SERVING: 5**

**Ingredients:**

- 2 teaspoons pure lemon extract
- 3 tablespoons lemon juice
- 1 ¼ cups blueberries
- 1 teaspoon vanilla extract
- 1/3 cup canola oil
- ½ cup sugar
- 1 ½ cups whole wheat flour
- 1 cup soy milk, unsweetened
- ½ teaspoon salt
- 2 teaspoons baking soda
- 1 teaspoon apple cider vinegar

**Directions:**

1. Take 15 muffin tins and line them with liner. Preheat an oven to 350°F.
2. Take a mixing bowl (either medium or large size), add and mix in the vanilla extract, lemon extract, lemon juice, canola oil, salt, baking soda, soy milk, and vinegar in the bowl to mix well with each other.
3. Stir in the sugar and mix well. Stir in the flour and mix well; now mix in the blueberries.
4. Add the mix in the prepared muffin tins.
5. Bake for 22-25 minutes until tops are lightly browned and cooked through.

**Nutritional Values (Per Serving):**

**Calories – 124**

**Fat – 6g**

**Saturated Fats – 0g**

**Trans Fats - 0g**

**Carbohydrates – 19g**

**Fiber – 2g**

**Sodium – 347mg**

**Protein – 1g**

# Applesauce Bean Brownies

**Prep Time:** 8-10 min.

**Cooking Time:** 30-35 min.

**Number of Servings:** 12

**SMARTPOINTS PER SERVING: 1**

**Ingredients:**

- ¼ cup all-purpose flour
- 1/3 cup unsweetened cocoa powder
- ½ teaspoon baking powder
- ½ teaspoon salt
- ¼ cup applesauce, unsweetened
- 1 ½ cups black beans
- ¼ cup blackstrap molasses

**Directions:**

1. Lightly grease a baking dish (8x8) with cooking spray. Preheat an oven to 375°F.
2. Puree the beans in the blender and pour in a mixing bowl.
3. Ad and mix in the baking powder, salt, applesauce, and molasses.
4. Stir in the flour and cocoa powder; mix well.
5. Add the batter in prepared dish; bake until cooked through for about 35 minutes.

**Nutritional Values (Per Serving):**

**Calories – 143**

**Fat – 1g**

**Saturated Fats – 0g**

**Trans Fats - 0g**

**Carbohydrates – 32g**

**Fiber – 3g**

**Sodium – 263mg**

**Protein – 3g**

## Pumpkin Cake Muffins

**Prep Time:** 8-10 min.

**Cooking Time:** 20-22 min.

**Number of Servings:** 24

**SMARTPOINTS PER SERVING: 2**

**Ingredients:**

- 2 cups pumpkin puree
- 1 cup water
- 1 box yellow cake mix, sugar-free

**Directions:**

1. Take 24 muffin tins and line them with liner. Preheat an oven to 350°F.
2. Take a mixing bowl (either medium or large size), add and mix all the ingredients in the bowl to mix well with each other.
3. Add into the muffin tins; bake for 22 minutes or until tops are lightly browned.

**Nutritional Values (Per Serving):**

**Calories** – 89

**Fat** – 2g

**Saturated Fats** – 1g

**Trans Fats** - 0g

**Carbohydrates** – 17g

**Fiber** – 1g

**Sodium** – 126mg

**Protein** – 2g

Made in the USA
Columbia, SC
09 February 2020